**The Pronoun Book**
She, He, They, and Me!
**Cassandra Jules Corrigan**
**Illustrated by Jem Milton**
ISBN 978 1 78775 957 2
eISBN 978 1 78775 958 9

**The Big Book of LGBTQ+ Activities**
Teaching Children about Gender Identity,
Sexuality, Relationships and Different Families
**Amie Taylor**
**Illustrated by Liza Stevens**
ISBN 978 1 78775 337 2
eISBN 978 1 78775 338 9

**Who Are You?**
The Kid's Guide to Gender Identity
**Brook Pessin-Whedbee**
**Illustrated by Naomi Bardoff**
ISBN 978 1 78592 728 7
eISBN 978 1 78450 580 6

**ABC of Gender Identity**
**Devika Dalal**
ISBN 978 1 78775 808 7
eISBN 978 1 78775 809 4

# THE BIG BOOK OF PRIDE FLAGS

ILLUSTRATED BY
JEM MILTON

Jessica Kingsley Publishers
London and Philadelphia

First published in Great Britain in 2022 by Jessica Kingsley Publishers
An imprint of Hodder & Stoughton Ltd
An Hachette Company

1

Front cover image source: Jem Milton

A CIP catalogue record for this title is available from the British Library
and the Library of Congress

ISBN 978 1 83997 258 4
eISBN 978 1 83997 259 1

Printed and bound in China by Leo Paper Products Ltd

Jessica Kingsley Publishers' policy is to use papers that are natural,
renewable, and recyclable products and made from wood grown in sustainable
forests. The logging and manufacturing processes are expected to conform
to the environmental regulations of the country of origin.

Jessica Kingsley Publishers
Carmelite House
50 Victoria Embankment
London EC4Y 0DZ

www.jkp.com

THE **GILBERT BAKER** *PRIDE FLAG*

The first Pride flag was created by Gilbert Baker in 1978.

Gilbert had been asked by Harvey Milk, an LGBTQIA+ rights activist and politician, to create a flag for the LGBTQIA+ community.

Gilbert created a rainbow flag with eight colors. The colors of the flag have the following meanings:

pink = sex

red = life

orange = healing

yellow = sun

green = nature

turquoise = magic

blue = serenity

violet = spirit

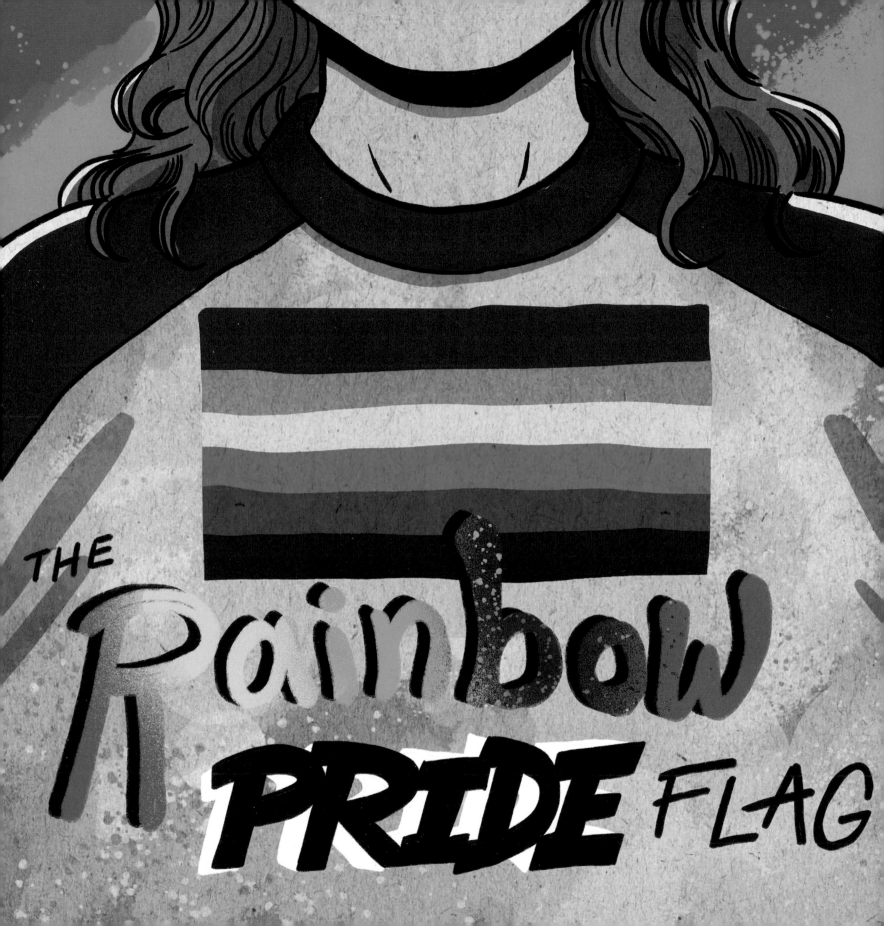

THE Rainbow PRIDE FLAG

The Rainbow Pride flag has become a powerful symbol for the LGBTQIA+ community across the world.

Based on Gilbert Baker's design, this flag has six colors: red, orange, yellow, green, blue, and violet.

Pink was taken off as this fabric was harder to find. Turquoise was also removed so there was an even number of colors.

In 2018, Daniel Quasar updated the Rainbow Pride flag to make it more inclusive.

The Progress Pride flag includes the white, pink, and blue stripes from the Transgender Pride flag and brown and black stripes to represent queer people of color.

The Agender Pride flag was created by Salem X in 2014.

Someone who is agender does not have a gender.

The black and white stripes represent an absence of gender. The gray represents being in between having a gender and not having a gender. The central green stripe is for non-binary genders.

THE AROMANTIC FLAG

The Aromantic Pride flag was created by Cameron Whimsy in 2014.

Someone who is aromantic may have little or no romantic attraction toward other people.

Green is used in the Aromantic Pride flag as it is seen as the opposite of red, a color linked with romance and love. White represents friendship and family and the black and gray stripes represent the sexuality spectrum.

THE **ASEXUAL**
FLAG

The Asexual Pride flag was created in 2010 by the Asexual Visibility and Education Network.

Someone who is asexual may have little to no sexual attraction toward other people.

The black stripe represents asexuality, the gray stripe illustrates the gray area between sexual and asexual, the white stripe is for allosexuals and allies, and the purple stripe symbolizes community.

The Bisexual Pride flag was created by Michael Page in 1998.

Someone who is bisexual is attracted to people of more than one sex and/or gender.

The pink stripe represents same-gender attraction, the purple stripe represents attraction to two or more genders, and the blue stripe represents attraction to a different gender.

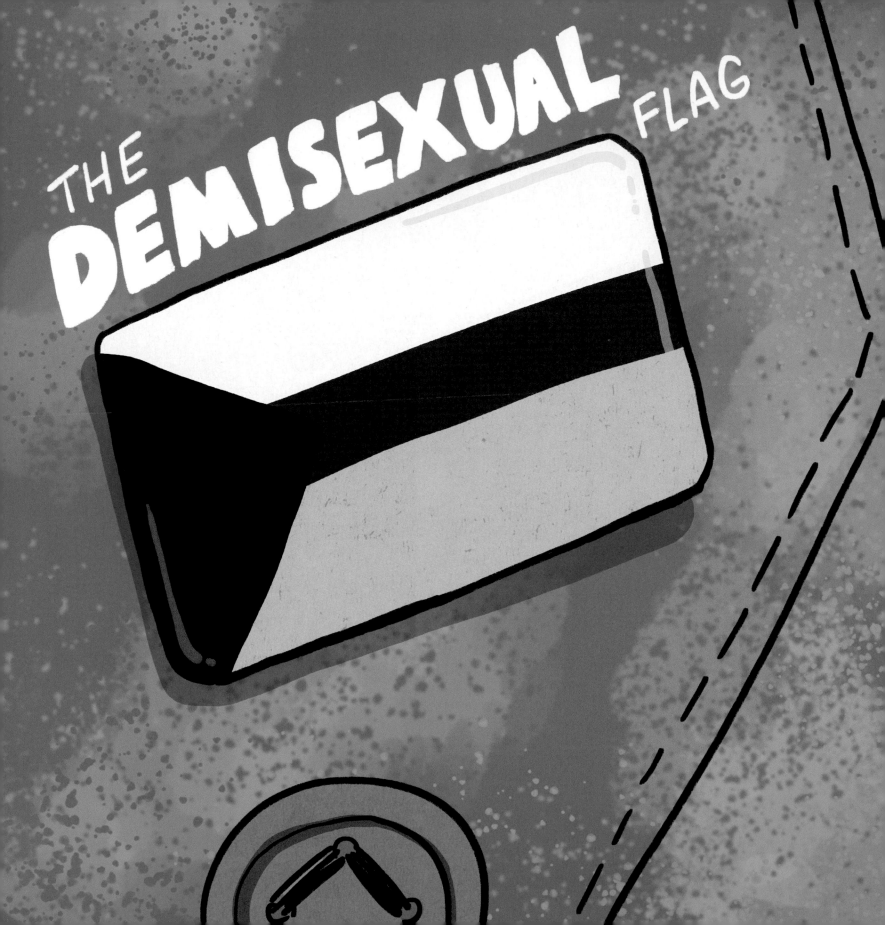

The origins of the Demisexual Pride flag are unknown.

Someone who is demisexual feels sexual attraction toward other people only once they have an emotional bond with that person.

The black stripe represents asexuality, the white stripe represents sexuality, the purple stripe symbolizes community, and the gray stripe is for demisexuality.

A gay man is a man who is attracted to other men.

The Gay Men Pride flag is inclusive of a wide range of gay men, including transgender, intersex, and gender non-conforming men.

THE **GENDERFLUID** FLAG

The Genderfluid Pride flag was created by JJ Poole in 2012.

A genderfluid person is someone whose gender identity is not fixed.

The flag has five stripes: pink for femininity, white for all genders, purple for both masculinity and femininity, black for an absence of gender, and blue for masculinity.

THE GENDERQUEER FLAG

The Genderqueer Pride flag was created
by Marilyn Roxie in 2011.

A genderqueer person is someone whose
gender sits outside of the gender binary.

The lavender stripe represents
androgyny, the white stripe represents
agender identities, and the green stripe
is for non-binary genders.

The Intersex Pride flag was created by Morgan Carpenter in 2013.

An intersex person is someone who was born with a body type that does not fit the typical medical definitions of female or male.

The circle represents intersex people being whole and complete.

A lesbian is a woman who is attracted to other women.

The first Lesbian Pride flag was created by Natalie McCray in 2010.

In 2018, Emily Gwen added shades of orange to make the flag inclusive of trans and gender non-conforming people.

In order from top to bottom, the stripes represent gender non-conformity, independence, community, unique relationships to womanhood, serenity and peace, love and sex, and femininity.

THE
NON-BINARY
FLAG

The Non-Binary Pride flag was created by Kye Rowan in 2014.

A non-binary person is someone who might experience their gender as neither exclusively female or male, or who is in between or beyond both genders.

The yellow stripe represents gender outside of the gender binary. White is for multi-gendered people. The purple stripe represents genders that blend male and female. Black is for agender people.

THE PANSEXUAL FLAG

The Pansexual Pride flag was created in 2010.

Someone who is pansexual is attracted to other people regardless of their gender identity.

Pink represents attraction to women. Yellow represents attraction to non-binary genders. Blue represents attraction to men.

THE *Polysexual* FLAG

The Polysexual Pride flag was created in 2012.

Someone who is polysexual is attracted to multiple genders, but not all.

The flag takes colors from the bisexual and pansexual flags and uses a green stripe to represent attraction to non-binary genders.

THE
TRANSGENDER
FLAG

The Transgender Pride flag was created by Monica Helms, a transgender woman, in 1999.

A trans person is someone whose gender identity doesn't match the sex they were assigned at birth.

Blue is for boys, the white stripe represents those in transition, or those who don't have a gender, and pink is for girls.

PROTECT TRANS YOUTH

# THE HISTORY OF THE

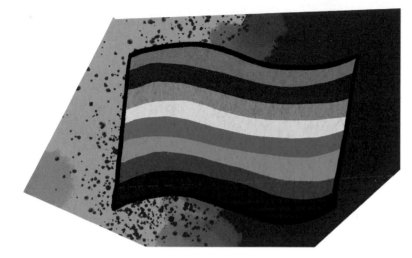

**THE RAINBOW PRIDE FLAG** has come to represent the worldwide LGBTQIA+ community and is a universal symbol of hope, courage, and love.

The original Pride flag was created by Gilbert Baker in 1978. Baker had been asked by Harvey Milk, the first openly gay elected official in California, to create a flag to represent the LGBTQIA+ community.

Baker wanted to create a flag that was positive and that celebrated love—the bright, hopeful colors of a rainbow were an obvious choice! Each color on the flag has a different meaning: pink for sex, red for life, orange for healing, yellow for sun, green for nature, turquoise for magic, blue for serenity, and violet for spirit.

# PRIDE FLAG

The flag was first unveiled at the San Francisco Pride Parade on June 25 1978. The flag was handsewn by Baker and measured 30 by 60 feet.

As the flag grew in popularity, the pink stripe was removed as the fabric was harder to produce in large quantities. Turquoise was also removed to even out the number of stripes. The six-color rainbow flag would go on to become the most well-known and used Pride flag.

In 2017, a brown and a black stripe were added to the traditional Rainbow Pride flag to better represent the experiences of queer people of color. This came to be known as the Philadelphia Pride flag, as it was launched as part of the "More Color More Pride" Campaign in Philadelphia.

As the LGBTQIA+ community continues to evolve, so does the Pride flag. The Progress Pride flag, created by Daniel Quasar in 2018, includes stripes for the trans community and for queer people of color. The most recent iteration of the Progress Pride flag also includes the Intersex Pride flag, further widening its inclusivity.

# READING GUIDE

☆ Which flag is your favorite and why? ☆

☆ Who designed the first Pride flag? ☆

☆ Which two colors appear on the Gilbert Baker Pride flag,
but not on the Rainbow Pride flag? ☆

☆ How many colors are on the Rainbow Pride flag,
and can you name them? ☆

☆ Why are these flags called "Pride" flags? ☆

☆ Why do you think it is important to learn about
the different flags and who they are for? ☆

☆ Why did people start making Pride flags? ☆

☆ Do you know what LGBTQIA+ stands for? ☆

☆ What does the flag you drew mean/represent? ☆

Use this blank flag to create your own Pride flag! If you'd like to download a copy of this page to print and color in, please visit **https://library.jkp.com/redeem** and use the code: **CAFHJYU**